KINGDOM † PROMISES
DEVOTIONS EMPOWERED BY BIBLICAL STATEMENTS OF FAITH

WE CAN

KEN HEMPHILL

B&H
PUBLISHING GROUP

NASHVILLE, TENNESSEE

KINGDOM PROMISES: **WE CAN**

ISBN 978-0-8054-2780-6

B&H Publishing Group
Nashville, Tennessee
www.BHPublishingGroup.com

Unless otherwise noted, all Scripture quotations
have been taken from the *Holman Christian Standard
Bible*® Copyright © 1999, 2000, 2002, 2003 by
Holman Bible Publishers.

Other Scriptures used include the New American
Standard Bible (NASB).

Dewey Decimal Classification: 242.5
Devotional Literature / Faith
Printed in the United States
3 4 5 6 7 09 08 07 06

I joyfully dedicate this book
to my brother and sister-in-law:

{ Phil and Elaine Hemphill }

Phil is the "big brother"
every little brother needs.
Phil and Elaine's
creativity and tenacity
demonstrate "We Can."

PREFACE

Studying God's Word always brings its own rewards. I have been deeply moved by the study of these simple statements that are scattered throughout the Word of God. It is my prayer that they will minister in your life as they have mine. I thank you for your willingness to buy this book and allow me to be your guide as the Holy Spirit informs your mind and transforms your heart.

As always, I am indebted to my wife, who is my partner in ministry and my encourager in this ministry of writing. She brings the order and solitude to our home that makes it possible for me to reflect and write. She is often the source of ideas that soon appear in my books. Our devotional times together frequently become theological discussions which enrich my understanding.

My children are a constant joy to me, and our growing family provides a rich context for writing. Tina and Brett have been blessed with a daughter, Lois, who is as active as her "papa." Rachael and Trey were blessed with a daughter, Emerson, whose smile lights up a room. It is a joy to watch Katie and Daniel grow in marital love and in the Lord. My family is the context for my entire ministry.

I want to thank Morris Chapman, the visionary leader of the Southern Baptist Convention for calling our denomination to focus on God's Kingdom. He has given me the freedom to write those things God lays on my heart. All of my colleagues at the Executive Committee of the Southern Baptist Convention have encouraged me in this new phase of ministry.

As usual the good folks at Broadman and Holman have been my partners in this ministry. I am challenged by the trust they place in me. Ken Stephens has led Broadman and Holman with integrity of heart. I can't begin to express my gratitude to Lawrence Kimbrough, my partner in this writing adventure. Lawrence is far more than an editor. He is a friend, colleague, and artist. What he does with a rough draft is a thing of beauty.

This book is somewhat of a new genre. It looks like a daily devotional in its format, but it is written to be "bite-sized" theology. I have attempted to explain each of these great Kingdom Promises in its original context and then to apply it to life. Thus, I highly recommend that you read this book with your Bible open, because the focal passages will have the greatest impact on you as you see them in context. You might also want to consider using these verses as a Scripture memory project while you're reading.

I pray God will use His Word to bring encouragement to your heart. And if this book of Kingdom Promises speaks life to you and ministers to your needs, I hope you'll pass it along to someone else.

Ken Hemphill
Nashville, Tennessee
Spring 2006

FOREWORD

My husband, Ken, is a "can do" guy. In this little book, he uses God's wisdom and scriptural principles to help seekers understand that "we can" do whatever God calls us to do, through Christ's power working in us.

In 1996 my father was diagnosed with stomach cancer. When he went to the hospital, he took a framed calligraphy of Phil. 4:13 with him. It sat on the tray by his bed during the entire eight weeks of his hospitalization and by his bed at home for the two weeks before his death. Dad insisted that in Christ we can die well just as we can live well. In all things, "we can" fulfill our purpose in God's plan.

Thanks, Ken, for living the truth in our home for thirty-seven years. Thanks also to those of you who will read these pages. May the Holy Spirit lead you to believe you can do "all things" in Christ.

Paula Hemphill

WE CAN
Experience God's Miracles

> **Genesis 17:17** Can a child be born to a hundred-year-old man? Can Sarah, a ninety-year-old woman, give birth?

One of the strangest phone calls I ever received as seminary president came from a lady who worked in a government office. She was inquiring about a man who had made application for his seminary tuition to be paid with funds due him because of his service in the military. I didn't see why this request would be any problem.

She then revealed to me the true cause for her concern: the gentleman was in his *eighties!* So her question was, "Could a man this old really have a valid ministry when he graduated?" I reminded her that Abraham was significantly older than eighty when he started his family. Fortunately, she knew the Bible and had a good sense of humor . . . and approved the old man's application!

The idea that a son could be born to an elderly, barren couple caused Abraham to fall on his face and laugh. But this promise of a child was accompanied by God's

revelation of himself as El-Shaddai—
"God Almighty" (v. 1). This name under-
lines God's sufficiency, and it was intended
to provide the reassurance Abram needed
to expect God's miraculous intervention.

But as an additional sign of his faithfulness, God also gave a new name to Abram.
Imagine what a reproach it had been for a
man with no children to be named Abram,
a name meaning "exalted father." God's
new name for him, however, was even more
unsettling—Abraham—meaning "a father
of *multitudes*." There's no question, then,
that Abraham's laughter sprang from his
unbelief. This is confirmed by Abraham's
suggestion (v. 18) that Ishmael, his son by
the slave girl Hagar, would make a much
more reasonable solution.

Isn't it wonderful that God is not
hard on his children when they experience
genuine faith struggles? Abraham truly
became a great man of faith, though he
certainly had days when he doubted.
Where do you need to experience God's
miraculous intervention? Are you willing
to accept his provision even if it differs
from what you expect?

WE CAN
Bless Our Children

> **Genesis 27:7** . . . so that
> I can bless you in the Lord's
> presence before I die.

One of the things I love about God's Word is that it accurately records the history of his people — warts and all — without trying to conceal the failings of some of its primary characters. In the familiar birthright-selling story of Jacob and Esau, for example, each player in the drama — both brothers and parents — bore his or her share of blame: carelessness, deceit, favoritism, manipulation.

Yet among the many negative lessons to be learned and avoided from this Old Testament account, we shouldn't overlook a positive one: the power of the parental blessing. Everyone in the story understood the value of the blessing, and both of the boys desired it with all their hearts.

Yes, "we can" bless our children. If possible, regularly hug them and tell them that you love them, that they are special and unique. No matter what their age, affirm the qualities you see God growing in them. Point them to various Bible verses God gives you, perhaps even writing them on a 3-x-5 card and giving it to them.

I have a grown friend in Dallas who was the son of a committed missionary couple. One of his most cherished possessions is a set of cards containing Scripture and words of encouragement from his dad, given to him when he was a young man. His father is dead now, but his words of blessing live on.

You can also bless your children just by letting them be themselves. Avoid the mistake of Isaac and Rebekah, who showed love only to the child who met their expectations. All too often parents try to mold their children into their own image rather than allowing God to mold them into his. But every child is uniquely gifted by the Lord, and it is part of our responsibility as parents to help our children discover their God-given uniqueness so that they can use their gifts with kingdom impact. Children never outgrow the need for their parents' blessing. God wants to use you to be one of his primary vehicles of blessing to them.

WE CAN
Be People of Our Word

> **Genesis 43:9** I will be responsible for him. You can hold me personally accountable.

A seven-year famine had brought the nation of Israel to its knees. So in desperation Jacob sent a vanguard of his sons to Egypt to buy food. But lest they fall into harm, lest he run the risk of losing *all* his boys the way he had once lost Joseph (his favored son), he decided to hold the youngest boy back. Benjamin was staying behind, safe at home.

But as you recall, when the brothers arrived in Egypt and found themselves unknowingly in the audience of their kid brother, Joseph—whom they had thought to be long dead—they were ordered to return home and retrieve their younger brother, Benjamin. To ensure that they were properly motivated for the round trip, Joseph even held one of his brothers, Simeon, in jail.

Imagine Jacob's panic when only nine of his ten sons came back, bearing the news that they had been commanded to return to Egypt with Benjamin as well. Jacob resolutely said no. He'd rather go without food than endanger another of his sons.

Enter another son, Judah, who stepped up and took responsibility for the situation, declaring that if he were to fail to bring Benjamin home safely, he himself would bear the full brunt of the blame.

From here the story gets even more familiar. The group of Jacob's sons returned to Egypt, where Joseph eventually revealed his true identity. Then he shocked his brothers even more by expressing his forgiveness toward them, his confidence that "it was not you who sent me here, but God" (Gen. 45:8). "You planned evil against me; God planned it for good" (Gen. 50:20).

But can you imagine what might have happened if Judah hadn't played his role, if he had not chosen to keep his word and be personally accountable to his father? His integrity at a key turning point in history resulted in Joseph's ability to rescue his family from destruction. So never discount even the smallest act of integrity. You never know what can happen as a result.

WE CAN
Exceed Our Natural Abilities

> **Exodus 4:17** Take this staff in your hand that you will perform the signs with.

This title should not surprise us, but it does. The Christian life is by definition a supernatural one. It is not merely *difficult* to live for God; it is *impossible* when we attempt to do it in human strength.

Moses began discovering this "we can" truth at the site of the burning bush, when God told him that he had heard the prayers of his people, had seen their affliction, and was prepared to come down and deliver them from bondage. Moses surely must have breathed a hearty "amen." It was *about time* God made an appearance on behalf of his people.

But then came the stinger! God said to Moses, "Go. I am sending you to Pharaoh so that you may lead My people, the Israelites, out of Egypt" (Ex. 3:10).

Moses must have thought he was the least qualified of all men to deliver God's message to the pharaoh. And just to be certain that God was aware of his deficiencies, Moses recounted them to him one by one: "Who am I? . . . They won't believe me. . . . Please, Lord, I have never been eloquent" (Exod. 3:10; 4:1, 11).

But the Lord was gracious and patient, even to the point of providing an object lesson that Moses would never forget. He instructed him to throw his rod on the ground. When Moses did, his ordinary shepherd's staff turned into a serpent, then back into a rod when he grasped it by the tail. And this was the rod that God gave to Moses as an instrument through which he would perform his mighty deeds of deliverance.

Why do so many Christians spend their lives in the natural zone, doing only that which they can do in the strength of their own flesh? God wants to empower us to do *his* work in *his* strength. He wants to take ordinary people like you and me and provide us with extraordinary empowering to accomplish his work in such a manner that only he can receive the glory. When we submit to him in this way, "we can" truly do anything he desires of us.

WE CAN
Be Set Apart for God's Use

> **Exodus 40:13** Clothe Aaron
> with the holy garments . . . so
> that he can serve Me as a priest.

It is beyond my comprehension that the sovereign God of the universe, the very God who spoke the world into existence, desires to use me. I sometimes feel like the psalmist who cried out, "What is man that You take thought of him, and the son of man that You care for him?" (Ps. 8:4, NASB).

Yet this "we can" affirmation—that God desires to use us for his glory—can be found as far back as the days when Moses was setting up the tabernacle, the sacred tent where the Israelites met with God. After arranging all the articles in their appropriate places and dedicating them to the Lord, he turned next to Aaron and his sons, washing them with water and consecrating them so that they could minister to God as priests.

You may be wondering how all of this applies to you today. But before you conclude too quickly that this passage has

little relevance for your life, don't miss
the incredible truth to be learned from it:
mortal man can *and must* serve God.

In the New Testament, Peter took the
Old Testament image of the temple—the
place of meeting that eventually replaced
the tabernacle—and applied the language
of the priest to all believers. "You your-
selves, as living stones, are being built into
a spiritual house for a holy priesthood to
offer spiritual sacrifices acceptable to God
through Jesus Christ" (1 Pet. 2:5).

Yes, we all function in a priestly
capacity in the Christian community,
making ourselves available for God's use
in serving his people. Paul called himself a
"priest of God's good news" and considered
his ministry "sanctified by the Holy Spirit"
(Rom. 15:16). The writer of Hebrews
extended this terminology to us, encouraging all God's people to "continually offer up
to God a sacrifice of praise . . . to do good
and to share, for God is pleased with such
sacrifices (Heb. 13:15–16).

Isn't it exciting to know we can serve
the Lord in a manner that has already been
declared acceptable and pleasing to him?

WE CAN
Enjoy God's Creation

> **Leviticus 25:19** The land will yield its fruit, so that you can eat, be satisfied, and live securely in the land.

This reminder of God's bountiful provision for man in the book of Leviticus becomes even more poignant if we pay particular attention to its context. Beginning with verse 8, the discussion turns to the "Year of Jubilee," when any land that had been sold reverted back to its original owners. This concept certainly sounds strange to our capitalistic ears, but the main reason why any Israelite ever sold his land was due to poverty. So the Year of Jubilee gave the impoverished Israelite an opportunity for a fresh start. In this way the land was never permanently sold.

And something else: it reminded the Israelites that all land rightly belongs to God, that it is his gift to man, a gracious expression of his love, given to us for our enjoyment and sustenance. We in turn are to manage it for God. Yet we, like many of the Israelites before us, have confused *stewardship* with *ownership*. We like to put down our property lines and declare, "This is mine!" But to discover true freedom and enjoy the fruit of the land, we must begin by acknowledging that it all belongs to God and that we are merely his stewards, held accountable to him for managing his resources.

You have no idea how liberating this can be! A couple in my church in Norfolk actually drew up papers acknowledging God's ownership of everything they possessed, even holding a ceremony to sign the documents. But not long afterward, their washer broke down. The husband confessed that in the past, this would have caused him great frustration and consternation. But remembering that he no longer *owned* the washer, he laughed in relief. He and his wife bowed down beside it and prayed, "Lord, your washer just broke. Now what do you want us to do about it?"

I have wonderful news! God has designed the land to yield its produce so that "we can" eat our fill and live securely. Take a walk today and thank God for his good creation. Enjoy it. He made it for you.

WE CAN
Only Do So Much by Ourselves

> **Numbers 11:14** I can't carry all these people by myself. They are too much for me.

    We all rejoiced at the pictures of toppled icons and freed citizens greeting the coalition forces after the liberation of the Iraqi people in 2003. Yet it didn't take long before some of the liberated Iraqis began complaining about the lack of food and resources.

    I guess some things never change.

    Moses certainly experienced this in his day. God had used him to deliver Israel from bondage. Yet the liberated Israelites had barely begun tasting freedom before they started complaining about its adversities. God had graciously provided manna to fall miraculously from heaven each morning to meet the people's need, yet the whining Israelites cried out for meat, bemoaning the free food they had left behind in Egypt. (Sounds like a released prisoner volunteering to go back to jail for the great food!)

It was enough to drive a man crazy! In fact, Moses himself joined the mighty chorus of whiners and began to question God, asking the age-old question, *Why me?* Finally, in utter desperation, he asked God to just go ahead and kill him now, if this was the way things were going to be.

God's solution? *Quit trying to do everything by yourself.* He instructed Moses to gather seventy men from the elders of Israel and bring them to the tent of meeting, where God would equip them with his Spirit to minister to the people. Creative solution, don't you think? We can only do so much by ourselves.

While the "we can" statements in this book are personally affirming, we shouldn't overlook the plural pronoun "we." Sure, God wants to use you as an individual, but the people of God are to live in community. Before you become overly distraught about all that you have to do, take a lesson from Moses. Choose some good friends to come alongside and help you in the task.

It is still true that you can do all things through him who strengthens you. You just can't do it all by yourself.

WE CAN
Overcome

> **Numbers 13:30** We must go up and take possession of the land because we can certainly conquer it!

I spent much of my early life involved in sports. I can still recall the locker room talks our coach would give us, psyching us up for battle. When he'd worked up the intensity level to a fever pitch, there was generally the butting of helmets and the slapping of each other's shoulder pads. (Sometimes I left the locker room with more bruises than I would receive in the game!) But just before we would charge onto the field, someone from the team would yell out a victory cry. We knew it! We could overcome!

Moses had sent the original spies out to the Promised Land with the same kind of locker room speech. Their job wasn't to make a yes or no decision about whether they could take the land or not. Their task was simply to determine how best to do it. But overwhelmed by the size of their opponents, the naysayers among the spies began to whine about the impossibility of the challenge.

I've heard the same kind of whining before: *I can't overcome this habit. I can't tell anyone about Jesus. I'll never be able to live the victorious life.*

You hear it in churches, too. *We can't afford a new building. We can't reach our neighborhood. We've tried, but the opposition is just too strong for us. We're just a little church.*

But into this scene of skepticism stepped the team captain, Caleb, who quieted the people with his simple speech. *We can overcome!* Tragically, though, Caleb's enthusiasm didn't win the day. The whiners' lying report doomed an entire generation to wander in the wilderness, perishing without ever occupying the land God had given them. But Caleb had been right. They *could* have overcome. He had made his assessment of the situation based on the promises of God, not on man's strength.

When you think about your ability to give, or to witness, or to live abundantly, do you believe that you can overcome? Hasn't God equipped you with his Holy Spirit to do just that?

WE CAN
Share God's Word with Others

> **Deuteronomy 5:27** Listen to everything the Lord our God says. Then you can tell us everything the Lord our God tells you.

If you read Deuteronomy 5 in its entirety, you will see an emphasis on the role of Moses as mediator. The people, shaken by the awesome voice of God that emanated from the flaming mountain, were concerned that they might die if they heard the voice of the Lord any longer. So they asked Moses to go near and hear what the Lord said, then to relay the message to them.

God doesn't speak from quaking mountains today. But each Christian has his or her own firsthand experience with God's Word. The messages he speaks to us as we read and hear the Scriptures are gifts from the Father, designed to encourage, correct, or instruct us in our moments of need.

But each experience we have with the Word can also be shared with others as the Lord gives opportunity.

In my early ministry I was called upon to preach many funerals and to offer comfort to those who had lost loved ones. I had been well trained in seminary. I knew all the right texts. I even had my pastor's guidebook with instructions on how to give comfort. But when my own father died, I will never forget the sweet words of comfort that came to me from the Lord through a "mediator"—someone who had been on the mountain of grief with the Lord and therefore could share God's Word with me from firsthand experience.

When God speaks to you in a specific moment, you become his mediator of that word to others. God may give you a special promise about raising your children. He may speak to you during your devotions in a way that gladdens your heart. And every time God speaks to you like this, you have the privilege of sharing that message with others. Like Moses, you can be the mediator of God's Word.

What has God said to you lately? Have you thought about sharing it with someone else? Don't underestimate the power of God's Word shared from one to another.

WE CAN
Turn Obstacles into Opportunity

> **Joshua 17:18** You can also
> drive out the Canaanites, even
> though they have iron chariots
> and are strong.

Everyone confronts obstacles regularly.
Some of them are of our own making;
others come from outside sources. They
may be financial, personal, or physical.
But the good news is that we don't have
to be limited by our obstacles.

One place to see this demonstrated
is in the above "we can" passage. All the
tribes of Israel had been allotted their
portion of the Promised Land. But the
tribes of Ephraim and Manasseh, being
considered together as a single entity —
"the sons of Joseph" (Josh. 16:4) — were
given only one allotment.

This clearly disappointed them. They
felt that they were far too populous a
people to be cramped and confined inside
land that was only big enough to accommo-
date one tribe. So Joshua said, *Okay, then,
go into the forest and clear yourself some additional acreage,* "there in the land of the

Perizzites and the Rephaim" (v. 15). *Use your blessing of numbers to your advantage*!

But the "sons of Joseph" began to whine and complain. They argued that there were too many obstacles. The Canaanites had iron chariots, and the Rephaites were considered to be fearsome giants (Deut. 3:11). They looked at the obstacles and failed to see the opportunity.

In 1994 I accepted the call to be president of Southwestern Baptist Seminary in Fort Worth. The school was facing several unusual challenges at the time. During chapel one day, I remember telling my Southwestern family, "Difficult circumstances are the platform upon which God demonstrates his supernatural activity." Truly, we often find God most at work in the challenging areas of our lives.

What enemy with "iron chariots" are you facing today? Do you have a forest of doubt and discouragement that needs to be cleared? Don't forget Joshua's words of encouragement to the children of Israel. You can clear the land and you can drive your enemy out. God is with you, and he empowers you to be an overcomer!

WE CAN
Be Strong in the Lord

{ **2 Samuel 22:30** With You I can attack a barrier, and with my God I can leap over a wall. }

I really had another title in mind for this kingdom promise: "We Can Leap Over a Wall." This reminds me of my childhood imagination, playing Superman, leaping over small obstacles but pretending they were "tall buildings." But this promise from 2 Samuel is concerned with *spiritual* strength and victory rather than physical prowess. David declared in this song of victory that the Lord was his strength.

Many of the images in this psalm are clearly military in their orientation, since much of David's life was spent in conquest. He compared God to a rock, a fortress, a stronghold, and a refuge. He recognized that his physical skills were in reality a gift from the Lord. Yet David also focused on the demand for personal righteousness. He spoke of God rewarding him according to the cleanness of his hands, underlining the necessity of obeying God's statues.

If you are familiar with the life of David, you may be wondering if he had forgotten his affair with Bathsheba and the cover-up that resulted in Uriah's death. How could David refer to his own righteousness and cleanliness? But don't forget that David was quick to acknowledge his guilt and repent of his sin when he recognized it. Besides, none of us should ever fall prey to believing that any righteousness actually comes from ourselves.

I know it may be possible that as you read this promise today, you feel like a child playing Superman. The idea of running upon a troop or leaping over a wall seems to be the stuff of childhood fantasy. But I want to assure you that you can be strong in the Lord. Your strength is not dependent on you or the size of your faith. It is dependent on the size of your God.

He is your strength! He is the rock of your salvation! As you acknowledge your sin, allowing him to cleanse your unrighteousness and help you continue in obedience, you will discover as David did, "He makes my feet like the feet of a deer and sets me securely on high places" (v. 34).

WE CAN
Leave Behind a Legacy

2 Kings 2:9 Tell me what I can do for you before I am taken from you.

Several years ago I had the privilege of preaching for a small gathering in North Carolina. This is my home state, and I always look forward to opportunities to get back to my roots. That evening after I spoke, an elderly gentleman approached me and said, "Sitting back there listening to you, I could close my eyes and hear your daddy preach. It's not just the vocal similarity. It's your passion for the church and your concern for the lost that remind me of your dad."

I have always considered that to be one of the highest compliments anyone has ever paid me. I had always known that my dad had passed on a great legacy, but perhaps I didn't truly know how much I had inherited.

The Old Testament prophet Elijah, in one of his final acts before being swept up to heaven in a chariot of fire, took off his mantle (sort of a cape, an outer garment) and struck the waters of the Jordan with it. When he did, the river divided at that place, and the two of them—Elijah and his younger associate, Elisha—crossed over on dry ground.

This is where Elijah spoke the words of 2 Kings 2:9, asking what he could do for Elisha before his mentor was taken from him forever. Elisha wisely asked to receive a double portion of Elijah's spirit, symbolized in verse 13 when Elisha "picked up the mantle that had fallen off Elijah" and returned to the banks of the Jordan, where he performed again the same river-crossing miracle. Much of the remainder of 2 Kings is filled with the strong accounts of Elisha's ministry as the spokesman of God and as the protégé of the great prophet Elijah.

You have a legacy to hand on to the next generation—the legacy of your faith and your values, the lessons God has taught you throughout your journey on planet Earth. Make sure that the legacy you leave behind in the lives of those who know and love you is a positive one that will impact others for the kingdom.

WE CAN
See the Light

> **Job 33:28** He redeemed my soul from going down to the Pit, and I will continue to see the light.

The book of Job is a faith pilgrimage in which he learns through suffering to see the goodness of God. It is a book that you should sometime read in its entirety. It reminds us that although complex issues cannot be solved with simple answers, God is the ultimate answer to all our problems.

The wonderful promise of Job 33:28 is found near the end of the book, of course, surprisingly located in one of the long, rather boring speeches of his so-called friend, Elihu. You remember Job's friends—the ones who came to him after his loss of family, health, and possessions and basically told him it was all his fault. These men could have easily been the inspiration for the famous phrase: "With friends like these, who needs enemies?"

And yet in the midst of one of Elihu's speeches, there is a nugget which must be mined. Job had asked along the way for a mediator to plead his case. Elihu pictured an angelic mediator — "one out of a thousand" (v. 23) — who would stand in Job's place, saying, "Spare him from going down to the Pit; I have found a ransom" (v. 24). Then Job's flesh would become "healthier than in his youth" (v. 25). Imagine what a precious promise this sounded like to someone who had faced the physical challenges Job had.

In response to this good news, Elihu imagined Job acknowledging his sinfulness (v. 27), yet rejoicing in the fact that God had redeemed him from the pit — the grave — an abyss as fearsome for ancient man as it is today. Truly, the only way to escape the awful specter of the grave and see the light is to receive the redemption freely offered by God.

These promises received their ultimate fulfillment, of course, in Christ. He is the Mediator who offered himself as a ransom, atoning for man's sin. Thus our flesh can be made new as we receive the new birth. This is the kingdom reality which makes the kingdom promise of seeing "the light" possible. Have you seen the light?

WE CAN
Tell Our Story to Our Children

> **Psalm 48:13–14** You can tell
> a future generation: "This God,
> our God forever and ever —
> He will lead us eternally."

It may be impossible for us to fully
comprehend the significance of Jerusalem
and the temple to the Jewish people. It was
a place of worship, a central focus of their
devotion, the symbol of Jewish pride and
culture.

In the psalmist's day, the sight of the
magnificent city of Jerusalem and its
central structure, the temple, would have
intimidated would-be conquerors. Yet that
same sight thrilled the hearts of pilgrims as
they approached the city. The faithful did
not see the ramparts as part of an impreg-
nable fortress to keep them out but as a
place established by God to offer them
protection.

The invitation to walk about Zion may
have actually been part of the worship
experience. It is possible that the officiating
priest invited worshipers to process around
the temple, observing its towers, ramparts,

and palaces. In this way they would gain an unforgettable impression of the majesty of this building which could be shared from generation to generation.

The temple, of course, was not to be the real focus of their praise. It merely provided the object lesson by which one generation could tell the next that God's presence and protection were as real as the rocks and structures they saw in their march about the city.

We should look for opportunities daily to tell the next generation about the character of the God we serve. If you have children, point them to the beauty of creation and use it as an object lesson to talk about God, the Creator of heaven and earth. Look for opportunities to interpret daily family events in light of God's sovereign care and protection. You can do the same with your friends and colleagues. Look around for visual illustrations of your relationship with God, and use them to encourage or witness to others about your God—"this God, our God forever and ever." We can and must tell the next generation.

WE CAN
Always Go to God

> **Psalm 71:3** Be a rock of refuge for me, where I can always go.

A few years before I received my AARP card (granting me "official" senior adult status), a friendly golf course manager looked at me across the counter and offered me the senior adult discount. While I liked the idea of getting cheaper greens fees, I must admit it hurt to be considered ready for it. Because after all, while the aging process does bring with it a few rewards, it certainly has its drawbacks. Our physical abilities and stamina erode. Our sense of usefulness can be questioned, and therefore our self-esteem can suffer. Loneliness and isolation are constant enemies.

The author of this kingdom promise understood this. He too was aging and he knew it. He cried out to the Lord, "Don't discard me in my old age; as my strength fails, do not abandon me" (v. 9). Yet despite such words—despite the reality of coming face-to-face with the fact that he had only a short time left on this earth — his was not a psalm of despair but of hope. Against the challenges of aging, he set his trust in God's faithfulness. He had experienced too much of it to doubt it.

In order to visualize God's help and protection, he used an image that would have been a familiar one to the hearers and readers of his day. In the open desert, a wind storm could appear suddenly and threaten the life of any traveler. But if a rock outcropping or a cave-like formation was nearby, a person who was faced with unexpected danger could find a life-saving place of refuge.

The psalmist knew that the Lord was like that — a haven, a safe habitation — a place where he could continually come for shelter, refuge, and retreat.

Have you discovered the Lord to be a hiding place as you face the challenges of life? Do the fears of aging cause you to lose yourself in worry? Rest assured that you "can always go" to God, finding in the strength of his Word all the sustenance you need to meet the difficulties ahead.

WE CAN
Answer the Critic

> **Psalm 119:42** I can answer the one who taunts me, for I trust in Your word.

Are you ever at a loss for words? More specifically, do you sometimes find yourself stumbling when asked about your commitment to Christ? I don't know any believer who hasn't been in that situation at one time or another. This wonderful kingdom promise, then, should give you renewed assurance.

The psalmist clearly stated the reason for his confidence in being able to answer the critic: "I trust in Your word." This may at first sound like a simplistic, unrealistic answer to a very complex issue. Yet throughout this great psalm, the writer actually gave us several key steps that enable us to develop trust in God's Word—and as a result, confidence in responding to the critic.

• *First, we must receive it.* "Teach me, Lord, the meaning of Your statutes," he wrote (v. 33). In other verses he pled to "understand" the Word (v. 34) and asked God to "confirm" what he read in the law (v. 38). He gave the Word his time and listened to what God was saying through it.

• *Second, we must appropriate it.* The psalmist welcomed the "faithful love" that came to him according to God's Word. He had not only received it; he had also embraced it. This appropriation of the Word naturally leads to our willingness to obey it—a constant theme of Psalm 119 that is most clearly seen in verse 44: "I will always keep your law, forever and ever."

• *Finally, we must delight in it.* Numerous references speak to the boundless joy and "pleasure" the psalmist felt toward the Word of God. He declared that he sought God's precepts (v. 45), spoke of God's decrees before kings (v. 46), and loved God's commandments (v. 48). The Word was his life, his food and drink.

When we develop this sort of passionate love affair for God's Word, we will discover that we too have the ability to answer our critics. Study God's Word faithfully, and in studying ask him to give you the confidence to speak with loving boldness.

WE CAN
Live in Unity

> **Psalm 133:1** How good and pleasant it is when brothers can live together!

The two pictures David chose in this psalm to underline the significance of unity may not be as moving to you as they were to the original readers. First, he compared unity to the anointing oil that was poured over the head of Aaron in such abundance that it would flow down over the edge of his robes (v. 2). The second picture was of the dew as it brought refreshment to Mount Hermon, the highest mountain in Israel (v. 3).

These two images tell us that unity is both fragrant and refreshing. They also tell us that unity is a result of God's grace. It is something given to us from above, from on high.

We cannot contemplate unity without thinking of the great high priestly prayer of Jesus. One of Jesus' final requests for his disciples was for their unity. He asked the Father to "protect them by Your name

. . . so that they may be one as We are one" (John 17:11), not just to make them enjoy each other's company but "so the world may believe . . . so the world may know" that God sent his Son to forgive sin (vv. 21, 23).

While unity is indeed a gift from God, it must still be maintained through our personal involvement. Paul exhorted the believers in Ephesus to be diligent to preserve "the unity of the Spirit with the peace that binds us" (Eph. 4:3). He then underlined a seven-fold basis for our unity: "one body and one spirit . . . one hope . . . one Lord, one faith, one baptism, one God and Father of all" (vv. 4–6). And he called upon the pastors and teachers to equip the saints with the goal of reaching "unity in the faith" (v. 13). Unity is absolutely necessary for the proper functioning of the body of Christ.

What have you done to enhance the unity in your family and your church? Is there anyone you are alienated from? What do you need to do for the sake of the body and to enjoy the fragrance and refreshment of unity?

WE CAN
Help Those Who Struggle

{ **Ecclesiastes 4:10** If either falls, his companion can lift him up. }

The book of Ecclesiastes can be a bit depressing if you don't read it all the way through. After all, one of the refrains of the book is the phrase "vanity of vanities, all is vanity" (1:2, KJV). Do you ever feel that way yourself?

By investigating such matters as work, pleasure, and learning, Solomon (the author of this ancient piece of wisdom literature) concluded that much of what we do in this life is motivated by self-interest and jealousy. Further, he supposed that death would prove to be the ultimate victor no matter what one accomplished in his or her own short lifetime.

Yet he came to a victorious and sobering conclusion. He instructed his readers to "remember your Creator in the days of your youth" (12:1), because wise living in every age mandates that we "fear God and keep His commands" (12:13).

Even in heeding this encouraging piece of advice, though, everyday life can still pound us down. So is there any good news to draw from all of this? Yes! It's found in one of God's little gifts to help us deal with problems like oppression, poverty, loneliness, and injustice: we can count on the companionship and assistance of others.

Solomon expressed this truth by using three illustrations that referred to some of the risks of travel in ancient days. While walking across a dark and unfamiliar piece of ground, for example, one might fall into a pit or ravine. Such a fall could be fatal after nightfall in a deserted area. The second risk came from cold, desert nights. Even in that kind of discomfort, however, traveling companions could share body heat and thus help each other. The third risk was assault by bandits. But where one person was easy prey, two could more easily resist the attack.

Even an enlightened self-interest warns against the isolated ego and points to our need for others. Kingdom minded citizens always look for community, helping those at risk in our cold, impersonal world.

WE CAN
See God's Word Fulfilled

> **Jeremiah 32:24** What You have spoken has happened. Look, You can see it!

Have you ever had buyer's remorse? Those television infomercials are infamous for creating desire for a product that you really don't need (or even want) until you see it advertised. On a whim, you pick up the phone, and before you know it, the three-easy-payment wonder is on your credit card and on the way to your home. The next morning, though, you wonder what possessed you to buy on impulse.

Jeremiah, one of the great prophets of the Old Testament had his own unique case of buyer's remorse. He bought a field from his nephew, which might ordinarily have been an astute decision except for one small detail: the Babylonians had already built siege ramps around Jerusalem.

Still, he hadn't tried to hide his intentions. He signed for his purchase in the presence of all the Jews who were sitting in the court of the guard. He gave instruc-

tions that the deed be sealed in an earthen-
ware jar so that it could last a long time.
That's because he had bought the field
based on God's promise that "houses,
fields, and vineyards will again be bought
in this land," despite the period of exile
that was upon them (32:15).

When Jeremiah was alone with the
Lord, he broke forth in prayer, combatting
his buyer's remorse with powerful praise.
He affirmed that nothing is too difficult
for God—the one who has always acted
according to the integrity of his own name.
Even looking at the siege mounds, he
declared that God's Word was being
fulfilled.

The "You" in the "You can see it"
of verse 24 probably refers to God, since
Jeremiah was speaking to him in prayer.
But no doubt it included the prophet, too,
who had just declared his conviction that
God was always faithful to his own
character.

When you make a commitment to holy
God that is based on his Word and character, you can see his Word being fulfilled as
he brings all of his promises to pass.

WE CAN
Live Only by Obeying God's Word

> **Jeremiah 38:20** Obey the voice of the Lord in what I am telling you, so it may go well for you and you can live.

Jeremiah the prophet was assigned the unenviable task of telling Jehoiakim, king of Judah, that the Babylonians were going to prevail against them and carry them into captivity. But when this scroll had been read to the king, who was reclining in his winter house before a blazing fire, he took a knife, cut the scroll, and tossed it into the fire. He thought ignoring the message would somehow alter the truth and change the outcome.

We face the same temptation. We read the Bible or hear it declared, and we are confronted by our own disobedience. How do we respond? We may not take out a knife and cut the offending pages from our Bibles. We may just do our cutting by simply ignoring them.

Jehoiakim ultimately paid for his disobedience by forfeiting both his throne and his life. His son, Jehoiachin, who followed him as king, ruled for only three months before being replaced by Zedekiah, a puppet ruler placed there by Babylon's king Nebuchadnezzar.

The tragedy of this story is underlined when one understands the meaning of the names of father and son. Jehoiakim means "Jehovah has caused to stand," and Jehoiachin means "Jehovah establishes." Who can calculate the missed opportunities that resulted from their disobedience?

You might think that Zedekiah would have learned an object lesson from the failure and disobedience of Jehoiakim and his son. It seemed so when he called Jeremiah and asked him to pray for the nation (37:3). Yet when Jeremiah warned the king that the Babylonians would return to lay siege to the Jerusalem and burn it with fire (37:6–8), Zedekiah responded by imprisoning Jeremiah, first in a courtyard and then in a muddy cistern.

Isn't it interesting that the leaders who consistently ignored the prophet's message would nonetheless seek his prayers? Many today do the same thing, ignoring God's Word while praying for his protection.

WE CAN
Ban Anxiety

> **Matthew 6:27** Can any of
> you add a single cubit to his
> height by worrying?

I frequently begin conferences on
The Prayer of Jesus with the question: "How
many of you would like to live the rest of
your life anxiety-free?" As you'd expect,
every hand in the house shoots up. Is it
possible to ban anxiety? Seems like a
pipe dream, doesn't it?

Yet Jesus asked his early disciples the
penetrating and revealing question above.
And we know the answer, of course: anxiety
does not *add* to our lives. Truth be told, it
probably shortens the life span of many.
Anxiety is connected to many illnesses, and
the drugs that combat its side-effects add to
the cost of living for many people today.

So if we know that anxiety doesn't add
anything positive to our lives, why do we
persist in doing it?

Five times in ten verses from Matthew,
chapter 6, Jesus banned anxiety in our
lives. He spoke of how it tended to arise

from real issues, like food and clothes, the length of our lives, and the events of tomorrow. On three occasions (vv. 25, 31, 34) he presented his ban as an imperative, thus commanding us to stop worrying!

Do you want to know how to ban anxiety?

• *It begins with a personal relationship with God through his Son*, which allows you to address him as "Father."

• *Further, you must understand that your Father knows what you need* and that he is faithful to provide you every required resource.

• *Finally, you must follow Jesus' instructions to seek first his kingdom and his righteousness.* When we place life's highest priority on worldly possessions, we will be fraught with anxiety. But when we focus on the kingdom of God, we will experience his provision and peace.

Surely Paul understood this when he instructed the Philippians, "Be anxious for nothing, but in everything by prayer and supplication with thanksgiving let your requests be made known to God" (4:6, NASB). "We can" live anxiety-free!

WE CAN
Produce Good Fruit

> **Matthew 7:18** A good tree can't produce bad fruit; neither can a bad tree produce good fruit.

If you go to the greenhouse and purchase a tree labeled "golden delicious apple," you have every right to anticipate that one day it will bear the luscious, yellow fruit that prompted you to buy the tree. You plant your tree and care for it as it matures. Finally, one year, you notice a yellow fruit beginning to form.

Yet you are surprised that the fruit remains small, and that the skin appears to be overly thick and its texture rough. Still, when the anticipated harvest day arrives, you fully expect to bite into the sweet juiciness of a golden delicious apple. Instead, your mouth rebels. Your taste buds scream. Apparently, the trees had been mislabeled at the green house. An apple tree could never bear *lemons*!

Our focal text occurs as Jesus has just warned his followers about the danger of false prophets. How would these new kingdom citizens know how to detect a false prophet? Jesus gave them a simple litmus test: Look at the fruit. Professions must be tested by practice.

That's because profession is easy, and Christian behavior can sometimes be produced by human effort. But who we are will ultimately be shown by the way we live over time. True Christian commitment will result in changed behavior.

While Jesus didn't specify exactly what he meant by "fruit," we would likely be on target if we looked at the fruit of the Spirit in Galatians 5:22–23. Oh sure, a Christian will definitely experience occasional failure, but the growing Christian will consistently bear the fruit that the indwelling Holy Spirit produces.

When we are born again, we receive a DNA transplant. We have our Father's genes, and we begin to reveal his character through our lives. Have you ever noticed that as you age, you begin to look more and more like one of your parents? The same is true for the Christian. As we mature in Christ, we will produce the good fruit of our Father.

WE CAN
Minister to the Needy

> **Mark 14:7** You always have the poor with you, and you can do good for them whenever you want.

Jesus was in the village of Bethany on the Mount of Olives, nearly two miles from Jerusalem. On this particular occasion, Simon the leper was entertaining him. While Jesus was reclining at table, a woman broke an alabaster jar containing pure nard and poured it over Jesus' head.

Those present at the feast reacted immediately. They obviously understood the value of the perfume, for they were indignant at what they judged to be a wastefully extravagant act. It was not altogether surprising that they suggested the woman could have sold the perfume and given the proceeds to the poor. (It was customary on the eve of the Passover to remember the poor with gifts.) But Jesus immediately defended the woman's lavish gift.

At first this may seem out of character, since Jesus sought no personal comfort throughout his life and ministry. There can be little question that the woman's act was one of pure devotion on her part. But Jesus saw it as appropriate precisely because of the approaching hour of his death. Apparently, the woman recognized that Jesus was the embodiment of the poor, and thus her gift was an act of both love and compassion.

Many people read this text and celebrate the generosity of the gift, yet miss the point of Jesus' rebuke. Since we will always have the poor with us, we "can do good for them." Jesus was not suggesting that we ignore the plight of the poor. On the contrary, he was suggesting that this woman's generosity should become a model of our extravagant concern for those in need.

Throughout the Scripture, God is shown to be an advocate for the poor, the orphan, and the widow. Numerous passages exhort the rich to share with the needy, and several Old Testament passages instructed God's people to allow the poor to glean the remains of their fields and vineyards.

What people are around you today, extending to you the opportunity to do good to them?

WE CAN
Be Ready for Christ's Return

> **Luke 12:36** When he comes and knocks, they can open the door for him at once.

All of us have had the experience of being left in charge of some matter, knowing that someone to whom we're accountable was returning soon.

Perhaps the most familiar scene is that of the husband left at home while his wife is away for a few days. This particular husband may not always pick up after himself on a regular basis. He plans, however, to make sure that the house is clean and ready for the return of his wife. The only thing that can spoil his plan is her early and unexpected return.

We know two things about the return of our Lord—it is certain and it will be unexpected. In fact, these two truths are asserted in verse 40: "Be ready, because the Son of Man is coming at an hour that you do not expect."

There has always been a fascination about the return of Christ. There have been numerous best-selling books that speculated about his return. Yet Christians shouldn't expend their energy speculating about the exact timing of our Lord's coming. Paul assured us that "the Day of the Lord will come just like a thief in the night" (1 Thess. 5:2), even for those who thought they had it all figured out.

Paul's emphasis instead was the same as that of Jesus in this passage: when the master returns, he should find his servants in a state of readiness.

Verse 35 speaks of the girding of the loins. That imagery is not one we are familiar with today, but at one time this was the first step in preparedness. The flowing robes of the men of Jesus' day were beautiful but not always suited for labor. Thus when one was preparing for work, he would tuck his robes in a belt around his waist.

The kingdom citizen can be ready for the return of the king. Prepare for that moment by offering your faithful service to him every day. As you serve the least of the brethren, you are also serving him.

WE CAN
Accept What We Can't Understand

> **John 6:60** When many of His disciples heard this, they said, "This teaching is hard! Who can accept it?"

You may remember as a child when your parents asked you to do something that you couldn't comprehend. Even when you asked for and received an explanation, the truth behind the request still remained veiled to your childlike understanding.

In truth, I daily accept and appropriate things I cannot understand. I am using a wireless computer to type this book, and when I'm finished I will e-mail it to my editor. I confess that I am clueless when it comes to technology, yet I accept the mystery and use it.

The sixth chapter of John describes a scene where people were unwilling to believe a truth they couldn't understand. After Jesus had fed the five thousand, the crowd wanted another miraculous sign, reminding Jesus that their fathers had been regularly fed by heavenly manna. When Jesus told them that it had been *his*

"Father" who had provided the manna in the wilderness, they were shocked enough at his presumptuous arrogance. But nothing prepared them for the assertion that followed: "I am the living bread that came down from heaven. If anyone eats of this bread, he will live forever. The bread that I will give for the life of the world is My flesh" (v. 51).

The Jews were reeling from this revelation of truth and began to argue among themselves like children. They had taken Jesus' statement so literally that they completely missed the symbolism of his sacrificial death. The idea that the Son of God would die to grant eternal life to man did not compute with their idea of the Messiah. It collided with their rational thinking and their own theological notions.

Many of those listening on that day left because they refused to believe. When Jesus asked his disciples if they too would leave, Peter declared, "Lord, who will we go to? You have the words of eternal life" (v. 68). Yes, we can accept the truth of God by faith, even though we may not now be able to fully comprehend it.

WE CAN
Share Our Testimony

> **John 9:25** One thing I do know: I was blind, and now I can see!

I was a college student, visiting in the home of a rather skeptical professor. We had presented the gospel to him, but the professor wanted to debate theological issues. It was obvious that he remained unconvinced and unmoved.

One of our team members, a rather shy young lady, sat forward in her chair and said, "I can't answer your questions, but I can tell you one thing: Jesus has radically changed my life." We all sat back and waited for his rebuff. To our surprise, he slumped back into his chair, stating that he couldn't refute her personal story.

In John 9 we find the story of Jesus healing a man who had been blind from birth. When the man's neighbors inquired about his newfound sight, he recounted the story of his healing. They took him to the Pharisees, who also wanted to know how he was healed. The Pharisees began to argue among themselves how a sinner (which they had concluded Jesus was) could work such miracles.

But when they asked the man what he thought about Jesus, demanding that he affirm their assessment, his response was simple and irrefutable: "I was blind, and now I can see!" Having shared his testimony, the young man became bolder in response to the questions of the Pharisees. He wondered aloud whether they too desired to be his disciples, seeing that if God does not hear sinners, Jesus must therefore be from God himself.

The Jewish leaders were enraged to hear a formerly blind man lecturing them about theological issues. They threw him out, frustrated at their inability to get to the bottom of this. When Jesus found the young man later and disclosed who he was—the Son of Man—he responded to Jesus, "I believe, Lord" (v. 38).

Your testimony is one of a kind and it is irrefutable. Sharing your testimony with someone else will actually build your faith. Can you think of someone with whom you can share your story?

WE CAN
Do Nothing Apart from Christ

> **John 15:5** The one who remains in Me and I in him produces much fruit, because you can do nothing without Me.

Many of the "we can" statements challenge us to be all we can be. They force us to grasp a larger picture of our capacity as a believer. They make us want to be all that the Bible promises we are. But I don't think any of the statements are as difficult for us to accept as this one.

Both our culture and egos dictate against our ability to accept the verdict of Jesus' clear statement. We might readily agree that we can't accomplish any of the *big* stuff, but we rarely accept the premise that we can't accomplish *anything* in our Christian life apart from him.

Oh, I know we can quote this verse with a sage nodding of the head. But aren't we often guilty of trying to accomplish things in our own strength? Then when failure is obvious we resort to the "I've-tried-everything-else, maybe-it's-time-to-pray" posture.

Jesus illustrated this principle of spiritual dependence by referring to an obvious horticultural principle. A branch is not a self-contained, independent entity. Separated from its life-giving vine, it is both fruitless and useless. It's the same way with us. Fruit bearing for the disciple is dependent on a constant abiding in Christ.

But how do we do this? How do we "abide" or "remain" in Christ?

• *First, we must develop a consistent and dependent prayer life.* Pray with the assurance that you are completely dependent on Christ for life and strength.

• *Second, feast on God's Word.* His promises to inform and guide us. You will find that God will speak to you through his written Word.

• *Third, get involved in a Bible teaching church.* The fellowship and mutual stimulation of other like-minded believers help us abide in Christ. Find an accountability partner who will pray with you about your intimacy with the Lord.

Yes, we can bear "much fruit" as disciples of Christ. We just can't do it on our own.

WE CAN
See from a Spiritual Perspective

> **1 Corinthians 2:14–15** The natural man does not welcome what comes from God's Spirit. . . . The spiritual person, however, can evaluate everything.

When you became a Christian, you received the Holy Spirit. And one facet of his ministry is to reveal the deep truths of God to his children.

This promise is best understood by starting with one of my favorite verses, 1 Corinthians 2:9 — "What no eye has seen and no ear has heard, and what has never come into a man's heart, is what God has prepared for those who love Him." Borrowing from two Old Testament passages, Paul declared that we can't even begin to imagine all that God has prepared for those who live in intimate relationship with him.

But then Paul declared that God has a way of revealing these things to his children, because the Spirit "searches everything, even the deep things of God" (v. 10). No unaided human could ever penetrate the unfathomable wisdom of God, but the Spirit of God knows these deep, remarkable truths. Just as no one knows a person's thoughts "except the spirit of the man that is in him" (v. 11), so the Spirit of God knows God from the inside.

It is this Spirit from God that we received when we were born again. And his desire is to teach us "what has been freely given to us by God" (v. 12).

Now, not everyone has this capability. The natural man is not equipped by the Spirit to discern the activity of God. His horizon is bounded by and limited to the things of this world, and no accumulation of worldly wisdom can make up for his lack. Have you ever tried to explain your spiritual values to your unsaved friends? They may smile and nod; still, they cannot comprehend the truth of what you are saying.

But the spiritual man—those who have been reborn through faith in Christ— can evaluate everything from a spiritual perspective. Yes, "everything"—both the secular and the sacred. We can make our business decisions, our giving decisions, our voting decisions—"everything"— based on the Holy Spirit who indwells us.

WE CAN
Become Wise

> **1 Corinthians 3:18** If anyone among you thinks he is wise in this age, he must become foolish so that he can become wise.

Some in the Corinthian community claimed to have special wisdom, which led them to arrogance and feelings of superiority. Thus Paul borrowed their language when he said, "If anyone among you thinks he is wise . . ."

Yes, they thought they were wise, and this spiritual pride and self-deception was at the heart of many of the problems in the Corinthian church.

Paul argued that the Corinthians were basing their wisdom on the prevailing trends of the age, comparing themselves against the wrong thing. He had already made it clear that current culture and its wisdom stands under God's judgment and is "coming to nothing" (1 Cor. 2:6). It was only the advent of Christ and his kingdom that had turned everything right side up. Yes, worldly wisdom is folly. That's why the foolishness of God displayed in the cross "is wiser than human wisdom, and God's weakness is stronger than human strength" (1 Cor. 1:25). In this new order, God's people may be nobodies in the eyes of the world, yet they really possess everything.

The fact that there is a new world order is not now plainly visible, but Jesus' cross and resurrection are evidence of its absolute certainty. Thus kingdom citizens must abandon their confidence in the wisdom of the present age if they want to become truly wise.

Here's the dilemma: many people who claim to be Christians continue to value the wisdom of the world above the wisdom of God. They attend church, but they live their daily lives based on the wisdom of the world.

Kingdom citizens, however, "can become wise" by considering foolish the standards of the world—by loving their enemies, turning the other cheek, going the second mile, and becoming givers rather than takers. Such godly wisdom seems alien to the wisdom of this age. But which do you choose?

WE CAN
Endure Temptation

> **1 Corinthians 10:13** With the temptation He will also provide a way of escape, so that you are able to bear it.

I can still remember the encouraging words of my dad as he treaded water in the deep end of the pool, positioned just under the high dive: "Come on, son, you can do it!" That's what this "we can" promise from Scripture is like: a word of encouragement for those times when we find ourselves facing the hard spots of life.

I do have a word of warning, though. We often apply this promise without paying attention to the original context, treating it like an insurance policy against spiritual failure, neglecting the fact that our own arrogance and disobedience are usually at fault for placing us in such a compromising situation.

In the first twelve verses of chapter 10, Paul used archival snapshots from Israel's past to warn his first-century listeners not to desire evil the way their forefathers had. He urged them to avoid the idolatry, immorality, and ingratitude that so often led them astray from God's best. Clearly, then, we cannot disobey God's written Word and then quote a Scripture like this as if it's a magic wand that will immediately whisk us away from our problems. Remember this: "Whoever thinks he stands must be careful not to fall!" (v. 12).

Yet with this word of warning in hand, we can grab hold of this reminder that we are not the only ones being treated to temptation and trouble, and that our ability to stand tall through our times of testing is based on God's faithfulness, not our own ability to endure. Notice the focus of the promise: "He will not allow . . ." and "He will provide a way . . ."

The imagery is that of a trapped army which escapes an impossible situation through a pass in the mountains — not a free pass, but rather a firm conviction that God will bear us through our testing when we are following him.

Commit this verse to memory, and you will find that the Father will often whisper in your ear, "Come on, you can do it!"

WE CAN
Comfort Others

{ **2 Corinthians 1:4** He comforts us in all our affliction, so that we may be able to comfort those who are in any kind of affliction. }

The ringing of the phone shattered the solitude of my study, and the message did nothing to repair the quiet. The doctors had discovered that my dad had a malignant brain tumor.

Dad had always been the picture of health, and I was totally unprepared for this grim prognosis. Over the next months my church family ministered to me in incredible ways as I watched my dad's earthly tent fold up, as God prepared a new heavenly dwelling for him.

As pastor I had always dispensed comfort to others, but now I was on the receiving end. Those truths that I had so easily expressed from the pulpit had now been poured out in my life. I was experiencing the reality of this one unassailable truth: our God is indeed "the Father of mercies and the God of all comfort" (v. 3). It was also at this juncture that I discovered another wonderful truth: God's comfort is not bestowed on us just to make us comfortable. It is given to make us able to comfort others. When I sit in the waiting room now with a friend whose family member is awaiting surgery, I can bring not only a scriptural word of comfort but also a personal testimony about it . . . because I have been there myself, and I have experienced it.

When I was president of Southwestern Seminary, several of our students were martyred in the shootings that occurred at Wedgewood Baptist Church. I will never forget the brief but elegant prayer of a Catholic priest, given at the memorial service held at the Texas Christian University football stadium. "Father, I thank you that you waste nothing!" Truly, our God works in the midst of everything for our good, giving us comfort so that we might in turn pass it along to others.

Everything you face in life will provide you the opportunity to know God's sufficiency. And in due time, the Lord will give you the privilege of sharing what you've learned.

WE CAN
Pray for Others in Ministry

> **2 Corinthians 1:11** You can join in helping with prayer for us, so that thanks may be given by many on our behalf.

My wife, Paula, and a friend were heading to Afghanistan to minister in that country. Paula has frequently traveled overseas, but this was the first such trip for her friend Tammy.

I remember Tammy's husband commenting that he knew he could pray for our wives while they were gone, but that it was sometimes difficult to see the results of prayer. I understood his dilemma. We want to "do something." And prayer often feels so passive, so optional. It can make you wonder if prayer even matters.

When we read the context of this wonderful "we can" kingdom promise, we note that Paul had been experiencing a level of suffering severe enough to make him fear that he might be killed. "For we don't want you to be unaware, brothers, of our affliction that took place in the province of Asia; we were completely overwhelmed—beyond our strength—so that we even despaired of life" (v. 8). This perceived "death sentence" had taught him that he could not rely on his own strength but that he must trust in God, who has the power to raise the dead (v. 9).

It was at this point that Paul pulled back the curtain and allowed his readers to glimpse into the heavenlies, where the spiritual battles are waged and where prayer is the weapon that brings victory. He declared that the Corinthians could join in his deliverance by praying for him. Paul knew that he could only be delivered by supernatural power, and therefore he understood the absolute necessity of prayer.

Have you ever noticed that missionary speakers regularly request that people pray for them? Many will tell you that they value the prayer support they receive even more than they value financial support. That's because they know that their work is spiritual in nature. They know their battles will only be won in the heavenlies through prayer. Yes, "we can" pray, and our prayers do matter. Kingdom people are marked by passionate, powerful prayer.

WE CAN
Understand Spiritual Truths

> **Ephesians 3:4** By reading this you are able to understand my insight about the mystery of the Messiah.

Have you ever listened to yourself complain that you can't understand something? Perhaps you've just purchased a new television with all the bells and gadgets, or perhaps it's that computer software all your friends are raving about. After a few feeble efforts to program it or run it, you throw up your hands and declare, "I can't understand this new technology!" That's when one of my girls usually asks, "Daddy, have you read the manual?"

Usually, I haven't. But that's a good question to ask of Christians who often complain that they can't understand spiritual matters: "Have you read the manual?"

Paul, in his letter to the Ephesians, declared that "by reading" what he had written, they would be able to understand the insight God had given him concerning the mysteries of the faith. Yes, it was a "mystery," but not in the way we usually think of that term, as if it's the twisted, convoluted plot of a novel. "Mystery" here means the eternal decision of God which had been hitherto concealed, but which had now been disclosed by the Holy Spirit.

This "mystery" about "the Messiah"—the truth that redemption had been made available through Christ for Jew and Gentile alike—had been given to Paul through the inspiration of the Spirit. And it's this same Holy Spirit who continues to speak through the Scriptures to us today, allowing us to grasp the realities of spiritual living.

The tragedy is that many Christians, when approaching the Scriptures, make the same assumption I made after reading the manual on my new computer. They think the language and length of the Bible is too much for them to tackle. But while I may not have the mind or aptitude to understand technological writing, I know I can understand Scripture, because I have the Holy Spirit to interpret it to me. And so do you. All you need to do is read it, and ask the Holy Spirit to inform your mind.

WE CAN
Stand against the Devil

> **Ephesians 6:11** Put on the full armor of God so that you can stand against the tactics of the Devil.

I attended a high school where football was king. So in my day, if you were a male with your name on the student rolls, you'd better have had a really good excuse for not showing up for fall two-a-day practices.

I suppose that's what motivated P.Y. to come out and be there—all one hundred pounds of him. We knew that it wasn't his nose for football that had brought him out to the practice field, not when he hunkered down for the first time in front of the blocking sled . . . without remembering that he needed to put pads on!

Many Christians, though, are a lot like P.Y. They line up against the adversary without any equipment, and then wonder why they continually face spiritual defeat. Paul insisted, however, that we can stand against "the tactics of the Devil" once we've prepared ourselves, once we've realized at least three things:

• *We must be fully empowered*. I love the Holman Christian Standard's rendering of verse 10: "Be strengthened by the Lord and His vast strength." Man, I like that. "Vast strength!" As Paul had written earlier in Ephesians: "I pray that He may grant you, according to the riches of His glory, to be strengthened with power through His Spirit in the inner man" (3:16).

• *We must be fully armed*. Paul speaks of the "full armor of God" (v. 13). The defense mechanisms he described probably came from that of a Roman soldier, including such things as a heavy leather belt, sandals, shield, helmet, and sword. This armor served not only to protect but to impress as the soldier stood prepared for battle. And every item was totally necessary.

• *We must be fully accompanied*. We've seen enough Rambo movies to think that one soldier can defeat the enemy. Not true! Nothing is more risky than Rambo Christianity. That's why the verb translated "be strengthened" in verse 10 is second person plural. A good Southern translation would be "y'all." We must all stand together, fight in his strength, and win.

WE CAN
Focus on Kingdom Priorities

> **Philippians 1:10** You can determine what really matters and can be pure and blameless in the day of Christ.

How would you like to have the apostle Paul pray for you? An awesome thought, wouldn't you agree? When you read the letters of Paul, you discover that he regularly prayed for believers in the early church. These prayers are embedded in his various letters, not only to give examples of prayer but also to encourage the recipients.

Many of his prayers began with a petition for increased knowledge (Eph. 1:17, 3:18, and Col. 1:9). Paul's interest, however, was not simply for people to possess a growing body of information but to embody a practical concern for effective kingdom living. His prayer in Philippians 1:10 actually contains *two* "we can" promises. One relates to knowledge ("so that you can determine") and the other to behavior ("pure and blameless").

The Greek word behind the first promise means "to put to the test and then to approve as tested." This is like testing currency to assure it's not counterfeit. Paul used this same term in Romans 12:2 when he declared that we can "discern what is good." But the ability to "determine what really matters" only tells half the story. The more complete idea is that we can *discern* and then *accomplish*. Thus it contains the idea of "know and do." The believer, empowered by the Holy Spirit and guided by the Word of God, can know and do those things in life which really matter.

That's precisely why our knowledge of "what really matters" should in turn enable us to be "pure and blameless." Both of these words occur infrequently in the New Testament. Here they function like two sides of the same coin. "Pure" indicates that our lives can be genuine and holy, while "blameless" indicates that our lives should be such that they don't cause another to stumble.

Are you tired of putting most of your energy into things that have little kingdom significance? You can determine what really matters and live in such a way that you are prepared for the King's return.

WE CAN
Do All Things

When I was called to be the seventh president of Southwestern Baptist Theological Seminary, the school was undergoing difficult challenges. Not long after I arrived, we were notified that we had been placed on academic probation for events from the past. We were facing challenging circumstances we did not create. When I addressed the seminary family, I made a statement that helped carry us through those troubled times: "Difficult circumstances are the platform upon which God reveals His supernatural activity!"

When Paul wrote to the Philippians, he too was facing challenging circumstances. His money was low. His strength was dwindling. He had reason to wonder if anyone cared. But circumstances for Paul provided an arena for spiritual growth. He had "learned to be content" (v. 11) though seasons of adversity, privation, hunger, and need. He had discovered the lesson Jesus told his disciples—the lesson every kingdom citizen must learn—to seek first the kingdom and trust God to supply the needs of the moment. Through the lean times and prosperous times, Paul had learned that his sufficiency was in the Lord.

Truly, it takes the "we can" promise of verse 13 to fully ascertain the thrust of the lesson Paul had learned: "I am able to do all things through Him who strengthens me." Paul was rejoicing in the fact that God had strengthened him to do all that God had called him to do. Thus the context of the promise is clearly fenced in by the will of God.

That's why we cannot flaunt the word of God and glibly quote this promise with a blank check mentality. Through all of his circumstances, both good and bad, Paul had learned that when he was in the *will* of God, he could depend on the *power* of God.

Have you learned the promise of God's sufficiency? If circumstances are dictating your joy, ask God to show you his purpose for your present circumstances and to give you the power to fulfill his will.

WE CAN
Be Fully Assured

> **Colossians 4:12** You can stand mature and fully assured in everything God wills.

The believers in Colossae were being put to the test by false teachers, who were apparently basing their teaching on visions, insisting on ascetic practices, and advocating the worship of angels (2:16–18). It was enough to make Paul concerned that his Colossian brothers would lose their confidence in what Christ had done in them.

But among the things the Colossian church had on their side was one of Paul's fellow workers named Epaphras, a native of this ancient Greek city who had been an evangelist there. Epaphras was always "contending" for his people in his prayers (v. 12), a word that literally means "to struggle," pointing to the zeal and intensity of Epaphras's prayer life.

The content of his prayer is the point of this "we can" promise. He understood the destructive nature of false doctrine and the practical ramifications of deviating from

KINGDOM † PROMISES

truth. He knew that right doctrine is the foundation for right behavior.

So he prayed that his Colossian friends would be "mature" and complete, the same goal Paul was working for as hard as he could . . . "striving with [God's] strength that works powerfully in me" (1:29).

This progress to maturity is further defined by the prayer that they would be "fully assured in everything God wills." Epaphras knew that the Colossians were being tempted to seek maturity and perfection through empty philosophies and claims of special revelation. Epaphras prayed that they would discover (as each of us must) that everything we need is found in Christ, who is the fullness of the Godhead. "For in Him the entire fullness of God's nature dwells bodily, and you have been filled by Him, who is head over every ruler and authority" (2:9–10).

There has been a tendency in today's church to downplay the significance of right doctrine. But *knowing* what we believe is essential to *living* what we believe. God's promise that we can "stand mature" is based on our being "fully assured."

WE CAN
Accomplish Kingdom Ministry

> **Colossians 4:17** Pay attention to the ministry you have received in the Lord, so that you can accomplish it.

Do you ever feel like you're in over your head? I'm not just speaking in general terms, but specifically in relation to your ministry for the kingdom.

The whole of Scripture makes it clear that every Christian is saved from sin and called to service. Kingdom ministry was never intended to be the sole domain of a few seminary-trained professionals. Nevertheless, we can still be overwhelmed by the realization that we are involved in ministries that have eternal consequences.

It's worth recalling that Paul wrote this letter to the Colossians from prison. Yet his focus wasn't on his own condition but on the welfare of others. If you look at the immediate context, you notice that Paul was conveying greetings from a number of his colleagues in ministry to the church in Colossae. I love it when Paul calls them his "co-workers for the kingdom of God." It always helps to remember that we are all in this together. While each of us has our own ministry opportunity, we labor together with others for this grand kingdom cause.

Our kingdom promise for today is found in a note of encouragement Paul sent to a young servant named Archippus. We know very little about him or his ministry. In Philemon 2 we discover that he was a member of Philemon's family. Some suggest that he was his son. And though we don't know any specific details about his ministry, it's entirely possible that his role with the church was at best a temporary and unofficial one.

Yet the tone of Paul's note clearly suggests that Archippus was in need of an encouraging word. That's something all of us can identify with. We all need mutual accountability and encouragement. Like Archippus, we need people around us to say, "Keep it up. You can do this. You can accomplish it."

Remember that you have been given the Spirit to enable you to accomplish kingdom service. So ask yourself: What is it that you need to give attention to today?

WE CAN
Take Nothing with Us

> **1 Timothy 6:7** We brought nothing into the world, and we can take nothing out.

At first appearance this may appear to be little more than a solemn reminder that life is transitory and death is certain. But if you look more closely at the context, you will find a wonderful kingdom truth—the ability to live with contentment and see worldly possessions in a whole new light.

In this letter to Timothy, Paul was forced to deal with false teachers whose doctrine was not only upsetting the church but was producing disputes, divisions, and constant disagreements. At the heart of their teaching was the idea that "godliness is a way to material gain" (v. 5). There are still those, of course, who trouble the church today with the suggestion that the truly godly should never face illness or want.

Paul affirmed the believer's need for godliness, of course, but he underlined his appeal by quoting an axiomatic saying, insisting that "godliness with contentment is a great gain" (v. 6). Fundamentally, this declares a logical truth: just as material possessions were irrelevant at our entrance into the world, they will be equally irrelevant at the moment of our exit.

Why did Paul need to remind his readers of something so obvious?

First, he wanted to challenge those people who felt as though their earthly existence derived its meaning from the amount of things they could accumulate. This thinking continues to plunge people into ruin and destruction today, "for the love of money is a root of all kinds of evil" (v. 10). And among its most telling dangers is this: "By craving it, some have wandered away from the faith and pierced themselves with many pains" (v. 10).

Secondly, Paul wanted to put a positive spin on this for the kingdom-minded person. How much better, he said, to see our possessions as gifts from God to enjoy, to share them generously, and to invest them in the age to come so that we can "take hold of life that is real" (vv. 17–19).

No, you can't take it with you, but you can send it on ahead.

WE CAN
Encourage Sound Doctrine

> **Titus 1:9** . . . so that he will be able both to encourage with sound teaching and to refute those who contradict it.

Virtually everyone agrees that one of the greatest needs of our day is integrity in leadership. Groups as diverse as government, business, sports franchises, and churches have decried the lack of effective leadership. Apparently, though, this is not an issue exclusive to our generation.

Today's kingdom promise is found in one of the letters we call the Pastoral Epistles. These were written to individual pastors of the early church, yet they contain information that was applicable to all the members of the church, both then and now. You might be inclined at first to think that this "we can" promise doesn't apply to you, but I would caution against such hasty judgment. All of us are leaders in some context. Even if you don't hold a position of leadership in your church, you have someone who looks to you and your example for guidance and direction.

So here's the good news: *we can encourage others with sound teaching*. In fact, any encouragement we give that is not based on the bedrock of biblical truth may actually be misleading and harmful. But through your study of God's Word and your understanding of sound teaching, God can enable you to lift others' spirits.

Unfortunately, we have seen a serious devaluation of doctrine in our day. Some church growth advocates argue that the modern-day man or woman is not the least bit interested in doctrine. I hope they are wrong! Doctrine is not a bad word. It is at the core of our very belief system.

Notice, too, that this verse provides a double promise. Not only can good teaching be a benefit and blessing to others, it also gives us ground for refuting those who contradict what the Bible says. False doctrine cannot stand when lovingly confronted with the truth.

Never let yourself feel defeated for not having the profound intellect to encourage and confront others. Our ability to help others is based on the power of God's Word itself.

WE CAN
Share His Holiness

Hebrews 12:10 He [disciplines us] for our benefit, so that we can share His holiness.

I can still remember sneaking down the steps to the basement to hear my dad punish my brother for cutting up in church. I suppose I must have received some small measure of satisfaction from hearing him being punished, since as his little brother I was often the butt of his jokes and the object of his torture.

This was all well and good until it came *my* turn to join Dad in the basement. I'm not sure that I believed his usual comment ("This will hurt me more than it does you"), nor can I say that I enjoyed being down there with him. But looking back I know that my dad was disciplining me with love and purpose.

This kingdom promise is found in the context of a passage that speaks about discipline. The author is candid enough to admit what we all know: "No discipline seems enjoyable at the time, but painful"

(v. 11). We would also recognize that earthly fathers are not always perfect in the way they dole out their punishments. But our *heavenly* Father is perfect, and therefore his discipline is always just and purposeful. He is constrained by his own nature to operate out of love and for our good.

What then, you may ask, is the purpose of God's discipline? Simply stated, our Father's desire for us is that we share his holiness. Since God himself is holy, and since he created us with the potential to participate in his divine life, he uses appropriate and necessary discipline to shape us into His own image.

While this discipline will not be enjoyable all the time, it *will* yield "the fruit of peace and righteousness to those who are shaped by it" (v. 11). God's purpose is to fit us for his kingdom.

Be careful, then, how you respond to God's discipline. Instead of reacting in anger, crying out that it is unfair or too severe, thank your Father for caring enough to correct and instruct. Be glad that he is preparing you for his kingdom.

WE CAN
Be Coworkers in Ministry

> **3 John 8** We ought to support such men, so that we can be co-workers with the truth.

In John's brief third letter (only 14 verses long) he applauded his "dear friend Gaius" for all he had accomplished for the brethren, even those who were strangers.

We may need to unwrap this a bit. Early Christian missionaries were totally dependent on the help and support of those in the Christian family. Travel was both difficult and dangerous in the ancient world. Yes, there were a few inns, but even Plato the philosopher complained that Greek innkeepers were more like pirates than professional hosts. Rates were high and the accommodations were poor. Hospitality and support from other believers, then, was an important issue to the missionary community.

John encouraged Gaius to offer these missionaries hospitality and give them generous support for their missionary journey, "to send them on their journey in a manner worthy of God" (v. 6). That's because declaring the gospel and honoring the name of Jesus is just as much a responsibility of the *senders* as it is of the *sent*. By supporting these early missionaries, Gaius was becoming a coworker with them.

Have you ever thought of yourself as a coworker with your pastor or a missionary that serves on a foreign field? Whenever you support them with your prayers and financial sacrifice, you too are on mission with them.

What a shame that too many Christians today look at their giving in terms of paying for the services they get from the church. I love to get cards from missionaries telling me what God is accomplishing through our ministry together. No, I am not there with them, but through my financial support, I am a coworker. And that's a meaningful role in our kingdom community.

William Carey, an early missionary, compared his work to that of a miner. He said, "I will go down, if you will hold the ropes." Let's be those kind of coworkers together.

Appendix

The promises of this book are based on one's relationship to Christ. If you have not yet entered a personal relationship with Jesus Christ, I encourage you to make this wonderful discovery today. I like to use the very simple acrostic — LIFE — to explain this, knowing that God wants you not only to inherit *eternal* life but also to experience *earthly* life to its fullest.

L = LOVE

It all begins with God's love. God created you in his image. This means you were created to live in relationship with him. *"For God loved the world in this way: He gave His One and Only Son, so that everyone who believes in Him will not perish but have eternal life" (John 3:16)*

But if God loves you and desires relationship with you, why do you feel so isolated from him?

I = ISOLATION

This isolation is created by our sin — our rebellion against God — which separates us from him and from others. *"For all have sinned and fall short of the glory of God"* (Rom. 3:23). *"For the wages of sin is death, but the gift of God is eternal life in Christ Jesus our Lord"* (Rom. 6:23).

You might wonder how you can overcome this isolation and have an intimate relationship with God.

F = FORGIVENESS

The only solution to man's isolation and separation from a holy God is forgiveness. *"For Christ also suffered for sins once for all, the righteous for the unrighteous, that he might bring you to God, after being put to death in the fleshly realm but made alive in the spiritual realm"* (1 Peter 3:18).

The only way our relationship can be restored with God is through the forgiveness of our sins. Jesus Christ died on the cross for this very purpose.

E = Eternal Life

You can have full and abundant life in this present life . . . and eternal life when you die. *"But to all who did receive Him, He gave them the right to be children of God, to those who believe in His name"* (John 1:12). *"A thief comes only to steal and to kill and to destroy. I have come that they may have life and have it in abundance"* (John 10:10).

Is there any reason you wouldn't like to have a personal relationship with God?

THE PLAN OF SALVATION

It's as simple as ABC. All you have to do is:

A = Admit you are a sinner. Turn from your sin and turn to God. *"Repent and turn back, that your sins may be wiped out so that seasons of refreshing may come from the presence of the Lord"* (Acts 3:19).

B = Believe that Jesus died for your sins and rose from the dead enabling you to have life. *"I have written these things to you who believe in the name of the Son of God, so that you may know that you have eternal life"* (1 John 5:13).

C = Confess verbally and publicly your belief in Jesus Christ. *"If you confess with your mouth, 'Jesus is Lord,' and believe in your heart that God raised Him from the dead, you will be saved. With the heart one believes, resulting in righteousness, and with the mouth one confesses, resulting in salvation"* (Rom. 10:9–10).

You can invite Jesus Christ to come into your life right now. Pray something like this:

"God, I admit that I am a sinner. I believe that you sent Jesus, who died on the cross and rose from the dead, paying the penalty for my sins. I am asking that you forgive me of my sin, and I receive your gift of eternal life. It is in Jesus' name that I ask for this gift. Amen."

Signed _____

Date _____

If you have a friend or family member who is a Christian, tell them about your decision. Then find a church that teaches the Bible, and let them help you go deeper with Christ.

KINGDOM PROMISES

If you've enjoyed this book of Kingdom Promises, you may want to consider reading one of the others in the series:

We Are
0-8054-2781-3

We Can
0-8054-2780-5

But God
0-8054-2782-1

He Is
0-8054-2783-X

Available in stores nationwide and through major online retailers. For a complete look at Ken Hemphill titles, make sure to visit broadmanholman.com/hemphill.